THE RED SOX FAN'S
LITTLE BOOK OF WISDOM

Books by Curt Smith

America's Dizzy Dean
Long Time Gone
Voices of the Game
The Red Sox Fan's Little Book of Wisdom
The Storytellers
Windows on the White House
Of Mikes and Men
Our House
Storied Stadiums
What Baseball Means to Me

Also available from Diamond Communications:

New Editions:
The Cubs Fan's Little Book of Wisdom by Jim Langford
The Cardinals Fan's Little Book of Wisdom by Rob Rains
The Yankees Fan's Little Book of Wisdom by George Sullivan
The Giants Fan's Little Book of Wisdom by David D'Antonio

THE RED SOX FAN'S
LITTLE BOOK OF WISDOM

A Fine Sense of the Ridiculous

Curt Smith

Diamond Communications
A Member of the Rowman & Littlefield Publishing Group
Lanham • South Bend • New York • Oxford

THE RED SOX FAN'S LITTLE BOOK OF WISDOM
Copyright © 1994, 2002 by Curt Smith

Published by Diamond Communications
An imprint of The Rowman & Littlefield Publishing Group, Inc.
4501 Forbes Boulevard, Suite 200
Lanham, Maryland 20706
Distributed by NATIONAL BOOK NETWORK
1-800-462-6420

The previous edition of this book was cataloged
by the Library of Congress as follows:

Smith, Curt.
The Red Sox fan's little book of wisdom : a fine sense of the
ridiculous / by Curt Smith. p. cm. 1. Boston Red Sox (Baseball team)—Humor.
2. Boston Red Sox (Baseball team)—Miscellanea. I. Title.
GV875.B62S65 1994 796.357'64'097 44610207—dc20 94-23541 CIP
ISBN 1-888698-50-0 (pbk. : alk. paper)

Manufactured in the United States of America

• Introduction •

Imagine two men stranded on a South Sea isle from Providence, Rhode Island, and Presque Isle, Maine. The strangers differ in age, race, religion, income, background, and career. Their common denominator is the Boston Red Sox.

One day in late 1988, I visited A. Bartlett Giamatti at his New York office. I said that I was a Nixon Republican and a Red Sox fan and asked, "Does that bespeak masochism or loyalty?"

Giamatti sat back and roared his teddy bear of a laugh. "Clearly," he said, "it speaks of both."

The term Book of Wisdom may seem oxymoronic to the Red Sox fan. If we were wise, we would root for someone else. I beseech parents of young children not to adopt the Olde Towne Team. Life brings enough heartache as it is. Yet what evokes more love than New England's civic crucible? The Sox are grand and awful, stirring and infuriating, oft beaten and more oft self-defeating—but they are ours.

Like any relative, the Sox rouse a Rubik's Cube of memory. Thus, this 101-entry mix of fact, quote, and lesson. Think of it as prelude—like 1946 treking to '48-49 which led through 1967 to 1978 and '86. Reading this revised third edition, jot your entry down and mail it to me (PO Box 88, South Bend, Indiana 46624). In the sequel, full credit and a free copy will go to the author of each contribution—more than you ever got, say, from Cal Koonce or Kevin Mitchell.

A Dublin ballad says, "Being Irish means laughing at life, knowing that in the end life will break your heart." Ask fans in Southington, Connecticut, friends in Nashua, New Hampshire, or my mother born 40 miles from Boston. Being Irish is a lark vs. brooking Bob Bolin, Willard Nixon, Jerry Casale, and Willie Tasby.

—Curt Smith
Rochester, New York, and Blue Hill, Maine

(Un)sad, but true.

"When I was seven years old, my father took me to Fenway Park for the first time, and as I grew up I knew that as a building it was on the level of Mount Olympus, the Pyramid at Giza, the nation's capitol, the czar's Winter Palace, and the Louvre—except, of course, that it was better than all those inconsequential places."
—A. Bartlett Giamatti, 1988

The more things change . . .

. . . the more baseball stays the same. In 1911, the American League was trying to shorten games. One day, before outfielders were ready, Red Sox pitcher Ed Karger threw a pitch that the A's Stuffy McInnis lined to right field. Shades of Jim Rice: Thinking it was a warm-up toss, Boston outfielders failed to run—the result, an inside-the-park home run.

Think about tomorrow.

Before Fenway Park, the Red Sox played near a site where Bill Cody
later brought his Wild West Show. A great Boston fan-to-be,
"Nuff Ced" McGreevey, roared, "Who's going to play second base,
Sitting Bull?" He couldn't know about Pumpsie Green.

Timing is everything.

On April 16, 1912, the Sox dedicated their new home at Landsdowne
and Jersey Streets. They won its first game on April 20—
a 7-6 victory over the then New York Highlanders. Omen-watchers
were delighted: Fenway Park opened the week the Titanic sank.

I want a man with a slow (better, healthy) hand.

In the spring after Smoky Joe Wood's grand 1912, the 34-5 pitcher fell on his throwing hand and broke a thumb. It never healed properly. Watching movies, Joe couldn't lift his arm over the theater seat. Fast-forward to Carly Simon: Joe hadn't "got time for the pain." Nor the Sox for Wood—released in 1915.

Worry if, oh, say, he can't see.

Broadway producer Harry Frazee, doubling as Red Sox owner,
was the first owner to play *The Star-Spangled Banner*
before a baseball game—September 9, 1918. Let the
record show that Babe Ruth was then still a Red Sox.

Check what's in a name.

In 1918, Boston won its fourth World Series in seven years—
and fifth since the Classic began in 1903. Apropos of everything:
In '18, the first National Guard unit arrived in France—
the Twenty-sixth Division. Its moniker was "Yankee."

Morgan Magic

"Those games," Danny Ozark malapropped, "were beyond my apprehension." Ibid, Joe Morgan '88. Boston's interim manager won 19 of his first 20 games, took the A.L. East, and sounded eerily like Ring Lardner. "I'm the manager of this nine," he said—until the Towne Team fired him in 1991.

Friendship has its limits.

In 1919, Ruth hit a big-league record 29 homers. On January, 1920,
Harry Frazee sold him to New York for $300,000. He needed
the money to bankroll Broadway plays—among then *My Lady Friends*.
Noting the sign for one Frazee production flop, one fan said,
"Well, they're the only friends the SOB has."

Bathtub gin has its place.

Ruth's sale to New York occurred 11 days before Prohibition—
ironic, since it drove fans to drink. "You're going to ruin the
Red Sox in Boston for a long time," Sox manager Ed Barrow
told Frazee on learning of the sale. It did, and does.

Who needs *The Music Man?*

Aptly, Frazee's *My Lady Friends* was a farce. The Red Sox had won
five of the baseball's first 15 World Series. After selling Babe,
they finished last in nine of the first 12 Ruthless years—and won
exactly a single pennant in the next 47 years.

Tiparillos don't pay the bulldog.

Ruth was not reluctant to leave The Hub. "They had a Babe Ruth Day
for me last year, and I had to buy my wife's ticket to the game,"
he told reporters in the early 1920s. "Fifteen thousand fans show up,
and all I got was a cigar."

My Little Margo

In 1988, Wade Boggs' married ex-girlfriend filed a $6 million breach-of-oral-contract suit. Later, Margo Adams shed all in *Penthouse* magazine. Boggs confessed to sexual addiction. Fans shouted "Mar-go!" on the road. Only with the Sox.

Keep *No Way Out* in the VCR.

"I started at the bottom of this business and
worked my way right into the sewer."—Art Carney.
The 1925–30 Red Sox six times placed eighth in an eight-
team league. The box score: 311-603, and 292½ games behind.

Exception, not rule

Even Boston occasionally lucks out. It hosted Chicago on September 30, 1990. In the ninth inning, Tom Brunansky made a game-saving catch in the right-field corner to clinch the A.L. East. ESPN-TV's coverage scent more of Sox' tradition: It missed the play.

We all have fish to fry.

In 1928, rookie Ed Morris won a grand 19 of the Red Sox'
57 victories. He was a one-year flash—winning just 23 games
the rest of his career before being fatally stabbed by a
jealous husband at a 1932 fish fry.

"Green Acres Is the Place to Be."

Fenway's Duffy's Cliff was a 10-foot incline named after Red Sox
left fielder George "Duffy" Lewis. It was leveled after 1933 for a
37-foot-high "Green Monster" wall and later a 23-foot net atop it
to protect windows on the other side of Landsdowne Street. Sadly,
it couldn't protect Mike Torrez.

Call toll-free
A-r-t-h-u-r M-u-r-r-a-y

Smead Jolly once fell down on Duffy's Cliff while chasing
a carom off the wall. He told teammates between innings,
"You smart guys taught me how to go up the hill,
but nobody taught me how to come down."

The fault lies in ourselves, not our stars.

"That left-field wall was so close that if you were a right-handed pitcher and threw sidearm, your knuckles would scrape it."
—Vernon ("Lefty") Gomez, scraped less than most. He was helped, of course, by the team for which he pitched—the Yankees.

Uncle Dan

In 1994, New Englander Dan Duquette became general manager. He signed retreads, has-beens, and never-weres; wrecked the farm system; and inked every Chinese prospect save Chiang Kai-shek.

In 2002, new owners dumped the local boy not made good. Said a fan: "Next to Harry Frazee, he tops the Sox Hall of Shame."

Head Sox rhymes with dead flops.

On September 27, 1935, Boston trailed 5-3 but had the bases loaded, none out, and Joe Cronin at bat. Joe lined a ball that glanced off Indians' third baseman Odell Hale's head. It caromed on the fly to shortstop Billy Knickerbocker, who threw to Roy Hughes on second base for the second out. Hughes then threw to first—tripling Mel Almada—to complete a true no-brainer.

Imagine Jeffrey MacDonald as Skipper.

Boston's "Fatal Vision" sold Babe Ruth to New York, spurned Pie Traynor in tryout, shipped Bucky Walters to the Phillies, traded Red Ruffing for Cedric Durst, peddled Pee Wee Reese to Brooklyn, passed on signing Jackie Robinson, and later sent Jeff Bagwell to Houston. The Sox did, however, ink Ted Lepcio to a 1952–59 contract.

Know (or change?) thyself.

Players traded to New York were said to perform better in Yankees'
pinstripes. Away from Boston, even a new name helped.
Pete Jablonowski pitched horribly for the 1932 Red Sox.
Renamed Pete Appleton, he was 14-6 for Washington in 1936.

Welcome *Something Wonderful.*

Born in San Diego exactly 12 days before the Sox won their last
World Series, a rookie stood next to Bobby Doerr in 1938 spring
training. Doerr said, "Wait till you see Jimmie Foxx hit."
Replied Ted Williams: "Wait till Foxx sees me hit."

These bats are made for walkin'.

On June 6, 1938, Jimmie Foxx became the only A.L. player
to draw six walks in a nine-inning game. By dint of contrast,
center fielder Doc Cramer hit .302 in 3,111 Red Sox' at-bats—
yet smacked only one home run.

Don't worry, be happy.

Ted Williams struck out in his first two major league at-bats in 1939.
Ahead, two Triple Crowns (1942 and '47), six batting titles,
and his Everest .406 of 1941—and a niche as John Wayne
in baseball woolies for a generation of Americans.

Let's play "What's My Line?"

Ted Williams, Carl Yastrzemski, Jim Rice,
and Mike Greenwell all became Sox All-Star left fielders.
Name the fifth man: Good luck.
Unsung Bob Johnson, 37, in 1944 while
The Kid was in the Marines.

Birds of a feather . . .

In 1945, the A's Hal Peck made a bad throw that hit a Fenway pigeon
and deflected to the second baseman. The pigeon was killed, and
Sox runner Skeeter Newsome was tagged out. That same year, Boston
outfielder Tom McBride camped under what he thought was a long
belt by Sam Chapman. Too late, he found it was a pigeon.

. . . do flock together.

Like Sox pitching, Fenway pigeons beware. The Brown's Billy Hunter once hit a pigeon in batting practice. In 1974, Willie Horton hit a foul pop that skulled a bird. Ted Williams couldn't stand them—using a rifle until, unlike A.L. hurlers, the Humane Society stopped him.

Earning his keep.

Like many players, 1941–46 Red Sox reliever Mike Ryba played a different position in each inning of a minor-league game—and more. At game's end, he drove the team bus to the train.

"For better or worse . . ."

unites Red Sox fans. Winning 104 games, the 1946 club had
little need for a bullpen. So Mr. Ryba focused instead on hotel
lobby-sitting. In one month, he counted 35 weddings.

Teddy Ballgame (the good)

On September 13, 1946, Boston clinched the A.L. flag by beating
Cleveland, 1-0, on Ted's only inside-the-park homer. In Game Three
of the World Series, St. Louis manager Eddie Dyer left only one player
on the left side of the diamond—the Williams Shift. The next day,
a headline blared, "Williams Bunts!"

Teddy Ballgame (the bad)

In inning eight, Game Seven, of the '46 Series, the score was 3-all when Enos Slaughter scored from the first base on Harry Walker's double to give St. Louis a 4-3 victory. Boarding the train for return home to Boston, Ted forgot to close the blinds. More than a thousand fans saw him weep in his compartment. The reason—a .200 Series average for the greatest hitter who ever lived.

Himself (the ugly)

Williams was many things—but not a pitcher. On August 24, 1940, tired of Ted's boasting, manager Joe Cronin put him in for the last two innings of a 12-1 loss to Detroit. Ted gave up three hits and one run— and struck out Rudy York on a called strike 3. Underwhelmed by Williams' prowess, the Sox never pitched him again.

Have a sense of humor.

Philadelphian by birth and Victorian by bearing, Joe McCarthy became the manager in 1948. How would he treat Williams' spurning team rules by refusing to wear a necktie? Comically. Marse Joe appeared at a hotel in spring training in an open-necked sports shirt. "Anyone," he said, "who can't get along with a .400 hitter is crazy."

Know when to say no.

In 1998, opening Good Friday, the Sox banned alcohol for the first
time since Prohibition. Not everyone approved. "The only thing worse
than watching the Red Sox," said a fan, "is watching them sober."

Good karma doesn't last forever.

The Sox dropped a playoff for the '48 pennant. Next, 1949—
how could this ballclub lose? Four regulars batted more than .300.
Williams and Vern Stephens each knocked in 150-plus runs.
Don DiMaggio hit safely in 34 straight games. Mel Parnell and
Ellis Kinder, winning 48 games, were baseball's best pitchers.
It seemed so easy—till a season-ending weekend in New York.

Damn Yankees

On October 2, 1949, the Yankees and Sox met to decide the A.L. pennant. Trailing 1-0 in the eighth inning, McCarthy pinch-hit for starter Kinder. In the bottom half, the Yankees scored four runs and won 5-3. The two fought on the train back to New York, and each sought a flask. Said one teammate, "Ellie could drink more bourbon and pitch more clutch baseball than anyone I ever knew."

English 101 MIA

1997–2001 manager Jimmy Williams made Stengelese and Bushspeak seem a speech coach's dream. Jimmywock fused story, homily, and split infinitives, nouns and verbs. In 1999, George Steinbrenner criticized Williams. Jimmy replied, "When Georgie-Porgie speaks, I don't listen."

The longest day(s)

On July 12–13, 1951, the Red Sox and White Sox toured the land of
the Midnight Sun. The first night was a doubleheader. Game One
went the normal nine innings. Game Two lasted 17—and Ellis Kinder
threw 10 scoreless relief innings as the Red Sox won, 5-4. A day later,
Boston's Mickey McDermott pitched the first 17 innings as Chicago
won, 5-4, in 19 innings. No hurler was paid by the pitch.

Foretelling Roseanne

One day, the Sox' 1950–58 center fielder, Jim Piersall,
pretended he was a pig while leading off first base. It so rattled
Satchel Paige that the Browns' Ancient Mariner loaded the bases
and gave up a grand-slam homer to Sammy White.

Marcus Welby, phone your office.

Each Opening Day as president, Dwight Eisenhower threw out a first ball, which players scurried to retrieve. One year Boston opened at Griffith Stadium. Once hospitalized for manic depression, Piersall waited till Ike tossed the ball and gave him another as players fought for the souvenir. "Mr. President," he said, "would you sign this ball while those idiots scramble for that one?"

Experience must count, after all.

Williams said, "Baseball knows two languages—English and profanity." He preferred the latter in 2001. Somehow Williams kept the Sox in contention till August. Duquette then sacked him, at which point he hired novice Joe Kerrigan; whereupon Boston lost 26 of its next 38 games.

Ward, make sure the Beaver washed.

A Gallup Poll says more Americans would rather relive the 1950s than any decade of the twentieth century. Sox fans might disagree. In eight of the 1950s' ten years, Boston finished third ('50, '51, '57, '58) or fourth ('53, '54, '55, '56). Meanwhile, Wally, the Yankees won eight pennants.

Leave 'em laughing.

On August 7, 1956, Williams, who was booed for muffing a flyball, spat at fans as he neared the dugout, entered it, came out, and let fly again. Owner Tom Yawkey fined him $5,000. The next night, Williams bombed a long home run. Nearing the dugout—what a quipster—he whimsically put his hand over his mouth.

The Symbol

Of Boston's nearly 1,400 players, none embodied ineptitude more
than 1956 and '58–61 shortstop Don Buddin. Some said that Don's
license plate should read "E-6." Others said he had no license to play.

For No. 9, a one and a two.

In 1957, baseball's Lawrence Welk shunned Geritol to bat .388—
the majors' best since 1941. Williams hit 38 homers (one for every
11 official at-bats) and had a .731 slugging percentage. Only
Ted could mix Champagne Music and Narragansett Beer.

Let me make this perfectly clear.

For Sox fans hoping for a new era, this Nixon was not the one.
From 1950 to 1958, pitcher Willard Nixon won 69, lost 72,
and had a 4.39 ERA. (He did lead A.L. pitchers in '57 batting
average—.293.) Nor was 1960–65 and '68 catcher Russ Nixon
of the .256 Sox' average. Maybe they explain why Thoroughly
Modern Milhous three times lost Massachusetts.

Was "Ramblin' Man" dedicated to No. 4?

Let America have Van Johnson; New England had Jackie Jensen.
Beantown's towhead led the A.L. in run production the second half
of the '50s. Jensen had five 100-plus RBI years with Boston and
was voted 1958 A.L. MVP—then retired in 1960 because he hated
plane travel. A year later, he returned for a last act before leaving
baseball for good—by train.

Was Judy Collins a Red Sox fan?

In 1958, Williams showed his "Both Sides Now." He threw a bat, which struck a fan in the face—ironically, Gladys Heffernan, housekeeper of Sox general manager Joe Cronin. That Christmas, Ted sent her a peace offering—a $500 diamond watch. He also celebrated his sixth and final batting title—at 40, hitting .328, the oldest man to win a title.

Be grateful for small things.

On July 21, 1959, infielder Elijah "Pumpsie" Green broke into the Sox' lineup—ending Boston's cachet as baseball's last all-white team. Other first black players: the Dodgers' Jackie Robinson, the Indians' Larry Doby, and the Cubs' Ernie Banks. By contrast, Green hit .246 for the Red Sox.

Save the best for last.

On September 28, 1960, Williams retired as only a deity could—
with a home run, No. 521, in his final at-bat. The next morning
a Boston writer cried, "What are we going to write about now?"
On his last homer, Ted still refused to tip his cap. Later,
John Updike explained why: "God does not answer letters."

To Heaven and back.

Carroll Hardy was the only man to pinch-hit for Ted Williams
(September 21, 1960) and Carl Yastrzemski (May 31, 1961).
The outcome: Respectively, a double play, single,
and a changing of the guard.

"The meek shall inherit the earth . . ."

. . . but not the American League. In July 1962, pitcher Gene Conley tried to convince Pumpsie Green to leave the Sox and go to Israel. They got off the team bus in New York and went to the airport— where Conley bought a ticket for Tel Aviv. Providence then intervened. Both returned to the Sox to preach their Gospel of Mediocrity.

Dr. Strangeglove

The only people Dick Stuart terrorized more than rival pitchers were Sox fans and managers. One day, Stu got a standing ovation for picking up a wind-blown hot dog wrapper without dropping it. "Dick was 10 years too soon with Boston," said his 1963–64 skipper Johnny Pesky. "He would have been a great DH."

A little traveling music

In 1998, Boston withdrew Mo Vaughn's contract offer, demanded a psychological test, hired private detectives, and trashed Vaughn in the press. That November, what Dan Shaughnessy termed "The Black Bambino" left Boston. His destination: California, as far away as Mo could go.

Always take a paddle.

"I feel myself being drawn to television like a man in a canoe heading toward Niagara Falls." —Robert Young, 1953. The longer announcer Curt Gowdy stayed at Fenway Park (1951–65), the worse the Sox got. By five-year intervals: 400-369, 385-395, and a dreary 362-445. "For the record," Gowdy laughs, "I deny any cause and effect."

Youth wasn't wasted on this young.

On April 18, 1964, at 19, Tony Conigliaro wafted the first pitch ever
thrown him at Fenway for a home run. In 1965, he became the
youngest-ever American League home-run champ—'67, at 22,
the youngest A.L. player to hit 100 career homers. Next stop:
Cooperstown—until Jack Hamilton began his windup.

Pinch yourself—
you still won't believe it.

In 1967, Vegas dubbed the sad-sack Sox—ninth in '66—100-to-1
to win the pennant. Rookie manager Dick Williams said,
"We'll win more than we lose." By July, he said, simply, "We'll win."
On the final day, Boston won the flag to transport New England
and complete The Impossible Dream. Gushed Tom Yawkey on the
night of the pennant-winning, "I haven't had a drink in four years,
but I'll have one now." Millions still drink to *him*.

Me like 'em outcome.

One of Williams' first acts as manager was to let/make Carl Yastrzemski step down as captain. "We'll have only one chief—all the rest are Indians." Yaz found a better way to lead—.326, 44 homers, 126 RBI, and Triple Crown. Said catcher Russ Gibson of The Great One: "Nobody'd ever had a season like Yaz in '67. Nobody."—and nobody ever has.

61

Sun, Moon, and Stars

In 1999, Fenway hosted the Mid-Summer Classic. Before the game
Ted Williams, ill and frail, rode a golf cart from center field toward the
mound. All-Stars rushed to greet him. No. 9 and Mark McGwire
talked hitting. Larry Walker noted tears were in Ted's eyes—and his.
At 87, Fenway bid to tumble down.

Tunnel vision can be 20/20.

Reggie Smith led off one '67 tenth inning with a triple and later a second—but not before hundreds of cars backed up as a man refused to drive through a Boston tunnel until he heard the outcome. Many didn't mind: Outside the tunnel their AM radios caught every pitch.

There you go again.

In late '67, bad luck reclaimed the Sox. On a California mountain near Lake Tahoe, two days before Christmas, Cy Young Award winner Jim Lonborg fell while skiing and tore a pair of ligaments in his left knee. Like Joe Wood, Frank Baumann, and Jose Santiago, Gentleman Jim was never the same. By dint of irony, pitchers' legs/arms have been Boston's Achilles' heel.

Déjà vu can strike all over again.

Before the 1972 season, Danny Cater was traded to Boston for reliever Sparky Lyle. That year Cater had 39 RBI—Lyle, a league-leading 35 saves. Ultimately, Sparky won a Cy Young Award—Cater, a trip to oblivion. Twice burned (i.e., Babe Ruth), the Sox became shy: No Yankees' trade for the next 14 years.

Speed kills.

Sox' timing can astound. On October 2, 1972, the Sox and Tigers
started a three-game series to decide the A.L. East flag. Luis Aparicio
was on first when Yaz lashed a long third-inning drive to center field
at Tiger Stadium—sure to score the best runner of our time.
Ripley wouldn't believe how Little Looie proceeded to fall down
rounding third, retreat to the bag, and find Yaz there, too.
The rally, and pennant, died.

Hail to something old . . .

Richard Nixon said of the Great Wall of China, "This is a great wall." Ibid, the most famed concrete east of Beijing. Thomas Austin Yawkey died July 9, 1976. Fenway's left-field Wall still flaunts his and Jean Yawkey's initials in Morse Code dot-dashed on the green expanse near the scoreboard.

. . . and something new.

Yawkey padded the outfield wall in 1976 after rookie Fred Lynn
crashed into it in the '75 World Series. Lynn was the only freshman
to ever win the MVP Award (.331 average, 21 homers, and 105 RBI)
and seemed headed for Cooperstown. Maybe he should have
requested a Triple-A Triptik.

But Edward G. Robinson loved the Dodgers.

At 12:34 A.M., October 22, 1975, Carlton Fisk hit a 12-inning Series homer to win Game Six, 7-6, vs. Cincinnati—but how did NBC get the reaction shot of Fisk using hand signals and body language to force/pray the ball fair? Inside The Wall sat cameraman Lou Gerard—his task, follow the ball. As Fisk swung he saw a rat four feet away: "I didn't dare move, which is what I had to do to shift the viewfinder." Lou kept the lens on Fisk. The result of "You dirty rat" changed the future of TV sports.

You'll like the movie more.

1978 was not *My Favorite Year*. On July 19, the Sox were 62-28 and led the Yankees by 14 games. Boston then lost 9 of 10—and 14 of 16 after August 29, including four straight (September 7–10) to New York: the Sox were outscored, 42-9, ergo, "The Boston Massacre." It was a hint, they say, of things to come.

"Be yourself" is usually good advice.

Unless you're Don Zimmer. As Sox 1976–80 manager, he was a great third-base coach. After losing the "Massacre's" first three games, Yaz begged Zim to start Bill Lee. Hating Lee, Zimmer chose another lefty—rookie Bobby Sprowl—repeating, "The kid's got ice water in his veins." Sprowl didn't last an inning and never threw another pitch in a Red Sox uniform. Maybe it was tap.

Wendell Willkie was correct.

We are "One World." In Rome, the late Archbishop Humberto Medeiros used a recess of the College of Cardinals in late 1978 to ask a Boston television journalist how the Red Sox were doing. When Pope John Paul I died that year, a Boston TV station teased its upcoming newscast, "Pope Dies, Sox Still Alive." The Pope had never heard of Bucky Dent.

A stiff breeze can spawn stiffer drinks.

On October 2, 1978, the Yankees and Red Sox met at Fenway in a one-game playoff—prize, the A.L. East. For most of the game, the wind had blown in from left field. As Bucky Dent hit in the seventh inning, Boston ahead 2-0, it began to swirl out. Inheriting the wind, Dent's simple fly became a three-run homer. Final score: Yankees, 5-4.

Home sweet home

In 1999, the Sox unveiled their design for a new Fenway. It would seat 44,130, rise next to Fenway I, and cost $672 million. Would the park be built? Jimmy Williams shrugged. "I think I got the best shower in baseball. I'll take that shower and put it in the new park. The rest of it I'll leave up to them."

Fiddler's "Tradition" was better.

After Dent's homer, a New Haven bar owner moaned, "They [Sox] killed our fathers and now the sons of bitches are coming to get us." They still are, more than two decades later.

Be grateful for (un)small things.

Lost in Dent's thunderclap was Jim Rice's Great Year: 46 homers, 139 RBI, and 406 total bases in a major-league record 163 games— the only A.L. player to exceed the 400 mark in the last 63 years. Under consolation: Rice edged the Yankees' Ron Guidry for MVP.

Like "Maggie May," "Yastrzemski Song" is a classic.

In 1989, hundreds at Cooperstown sang Jess Cain's '67 aria. Yaz won 1969–71 Gold Gloves in left field—leading the league in assists each year. He went to first base for five years—then in '77 returned to outfield an errorless 140 games, lead the league in assists again, and win his last Gold Glove. Yaz holds A.L. records for at-bats (11,988), plate appearances (13,992), intentional walks (190), and games (3,308). All together, class: "He's the idol of Boston, Mass."

"The Man They Call Yaz" ain't mere lyrics.

After 1967, No. 8 was named president of the Arnold Bread Sports-
manship Club. Among its rules: "Success in sports—and in life—
is spelled 'hard work.'" "In '79, Yaz became the only A.L. player to
get his 400th homer and 3,000th hit. In 1982, another feat—at 43,
the oldest man to play center field. Yaz ended his career where it
began—playing his first game of 1983 (in its last game) in the
shadow of The (left-field) Wall.

"That Old Black Magic" ain't just a tune.

The retired numbers worn by Ted Williams (9), Joe Cronin (4), Bobby Doerr (1), and Carl Yastrezemski (8) hang on the facade overhanging right field at Fenway. What irony hath Red Sox spooks: Until rearranged, the epigram—9/4/18—recalled the month the Sox won their last World Series.

Here's to the old math.

In 1983, Cleveland scored twice in the eighth inning to take a 3-2 lead. Said Sox announcer Ken Coleman: "Here comes the tying run and the winning run, and the Indians win." He looked at the mound and saw Bob Stanley standing there. "It was then," Coleman said, "that I realized I'd goofed. Baseball is a nine, not eight, inning game."

Calling Speedy Gonzalez

In 1998, the Royals' Jose Offerman tied 13 triples and 45 stolen bases.
Acquired by Boston, he left his legs at the Massachusetts State Line.
In 2000, he had three triples, no steals, and was booed at Fenway Park.
Wags suggested that Jose change his name to Awfulman.

London can't match this fog.

Dennis "Oil Can" Boyd was a talented 1982–89 pitcher who was a bit, shall we say, on the blockhead side. One day a Sox game was postponed in Cleveland as fog rolled off Lake Erie. "That's what you get," said The Can, "when you build a stadium on the ocean."

Did Wade Boggs
like "Highway Patrol"?

"If you don't have a girl on the show, you don't have to shave so often." —Broderick Crawford, 1956. Wade outlasted Margo Adams' show/telling all about their extramarital affair to record baseball's most-ever (seven in 1983–89) straight seasons of 200 or more hits.

These are the good old days.

"In the '50s," said former Voice Ned Martin, "the Red Sox had great players cursed by mediocre clubs." In 1985, Wade Boggs won the batting title at .368—Boston's highest since Williams' .388 in '57. He linked a club-record 240 hits, 187 singles, and A.L. high 758 plate appearances.

CONTROL works—not KAOS.

In the 1980s, Roger Clemens recorded 38 double-figure strikeout games. No other Sox pitcher had more than 18 (Smoky Joe Wood). Maswell Smart would have rejoiced April 29, 1986. Clemens set a big-league record by striking out 20 Mariners—including a league-tying eight straight. "Chief, would you believe? Not a single walk."

KAOS works, too.

One day in May 1986, the Red Sox got 13 walks—but no one scored. In the tenth inning, Boston trailed by a run as Steve Lyons and Marty Barrett slid into second base from different directions. Stunned, outfielder George Wright threw the ball into the Texas dugout. Both walked home—as the Olde Towne Team won.

And away we go! —Jackie Gleason

On April 7, 1986, in baseball's season opener, off Detroit's Jack
Morris, Dwight Evans hit the first pitch of the year for a homer
at Tiger Stadium. It had never happened before—or since—
in major-league history. "How Sweet It Was!"—and remained,
till Game Six of the '86 World Series.

He who laughs last, laughs best.

With two outs, no Mets on base, and Boston leading Game Six, 5-3, in the bottom of the tenth inning—the Yawkeys on their feet in the dugout, the Shea Stadium message board prematurely blazing "Congratulations Red Sox," and Boston twice a single strike from victory—Bruce Hurst already picked the Classic's MVP and the Series trophy in the Sox' clubhouse—well, you know the rest. Whose fault? Ours—for not recalling the Red Sox as baseball's Heartbreak Kid.

Forget love and marriage.

Bob Stanley and Bill Buckner go together like a horse and carriage.
Game Six linked them then and now. Steamer's wild pitch plated the
Mets' tying run—Billy Buck's error the winner on Mookie Wilson's
dribbler. Fans remembered. Once, spotting Stanley, a Boston driver
literally rammed Bob's car. Buckner finally moved back west to
shake the ridicule. Ignore Laurel and Hardy. In New England,
sad-sack means another team.

The macabre has a certain appeal.

In 198/, Joel Krakow of the Captain Video Store unwrapped a shipment that included the World Series' '86 highlight film. Recalling Game Six, he knew where to place the baseball tape—the horror/science fiction section of his West Newton, Massachusetts, store.

You only make one first impression.

On April 4, 1988, newly acquired reliever Lee Smith yielded a
tenth-inning homer to Alan Trammell as the Sox lost their
home opener. Seeing it all before, the *Boston Herald* bannered:
"Wait Till Next Year." We have, and are.

Long Ball 101 was full.

On April 19, 1994, Mo Vaughn and Tim Naehring twice hit back-to-back homers as the Sox beat Oakland, 13-5. "Yes, the ball's been flying around the ballpark," Naehring said. "But whether it's juiced or not, I don't know. I missed that class in college."

Silver lining.

On April 12, 1994, Scott Cooper hit for the cycle as Boston beat
Kansas City, 22-11, the most runs allowed in Royals' history. "Yeah,
it's a little humiliating," said Kansas City catcher Mike Macfarlane,
"but you've got to look at the positive side. We scored 11."

Valhalla is no promised land.

Only five clubs eclipse the Red Sox' 34 Hall of Famers—
three executives, six managers, seven players of less than
200 Boston games, and 18 of more than 200. Who wouldn't
trade them all for a World Series ring?

If Baptism fails, try Benediction.

"Fenway," said Bill Lee, "is a shrine where people come for religious rites." Which Testament deserves Don Zimmer? Buried in a mock '94 ceremony, The Curse of the Bambino lives.

A horse is a horse—"Mr. Ed"

On September 20, 1995, the Sox clinched the A.L. East. After the game Mo Vaughn rode a police horse around Fenway Park. "I'll never ride a horse again," he later said. "Everybody was saying, 'You gotta ride the [police] horse, the horse is good luck.' The horse is *not* good luck." Vaughn went 0 for 14 in the first best-of-five Division Series.

Oh, Canada.

In 1996, Roger Clemens again K'd 20 in a game. That December, the Sox' greatest-ever pitcher bolted Fenway for the phony turf, devalued coin, and somnolence of SkyDome. "He's getting up in years," a Boston official said of Clemens. Apparently, not enough. At Toronto, Clemens won the A.L.'s 1997 and 1998 Cy Young awards.

Coming Attractions

In 1996, a '92 U.S. Olympic team walk-on homered in his first full big-league game. "The dream finally came through," said Nomar Garciaparra. "It could have ended right there, and that would have been enough." It wasn't. In 1997–2000, he blazed 113 homers, 420 RBI, hitting streaks of 30 and 24 games, and batting titles of .357 and .372.

Apocalypse Now

Sacking tradition, the '97 Red Sox unveiled a 25-foot Coca-Cola contour bottle design on the left-field light tower and Wally the Mascot, perhaps presaging Armageddon. A *mascot*, at Lansdowne Street and Yawkey Way? Next, Mo Vaughn would be asked to leave.

"The old ways are best."
—Ronald Reagan

Tell that to the Red Sox. In 1998, Boston broke a 13-game postseason losing streak—and still dropped the Division Series. The '99ers linked errors, runners stranded, and bad umpiring to lose the L.C.S. to the Yankees. We *had* been this way before.

Otis Campbell never went to Fenway Park.

"The funny thing is, I don't think I've ever been really drunk in my life."—Hal Smith as *The Andy Griffith Show*'s town drunk. 1946, 1948–49, 1972, 1974, 1977–78, 1986, and points before, after, and in between. Neighbor, go grab yourself a 'Gansett. Here's to New England's heirloom of the heart.

Pedro 'R' Us

(We hope.) Pedro Martinez was acquired in 1998. A year later he
K'd 17 Yankees in a game and beat Roger Clemens in the playoff.
The '99 Cy Younger blanked the Rocket, 2-0, in a 2000 ESPN
Classic. In the movie *The Razor's Edge*, Bill Murray said of life,
"There is no payback. Not now." Martinez's payback straightway began.

• About the Author •

Curt Smith is an acclaimed author, award-winning radio/television commentator, and former presidential speechwriter. He has written ten books, including *Voices of the Game*, the history of baseball broadcasting; *Storied Stadiums: Baseball's History through Its Ballparks;* and *What Baseball Means to Me.*

Smith hosts Rochester, New York, CBS-TV affiliate WROC's "Talking Point" and CBS Radio WHAM's "The Curt Smith Show." His daily radio commentary has been voted best in New York State by Associated Press and the New York State Broadcasters Association. Smith is also a columnist for upstate's *Messenger-Post* newspapers and senior lecturer in English at the University of Rochester.

Before entering radio and television, he wrote more 1989–93 speeches than anyone for President George Bush. Since leaving the Bush administration, Smith has hosted multimedia series at the Smithsonian Institution; written and coproduced three ESPN-TV documentaries based on his book *Voices of the Game*; and worked on ESPN's award-winning "SportsCentury" series.

Smith has written for the *Boston Globe,* the *New York Times, Newsweek,* and the *Washington Post.* The 1973 SUNY at Geneseo graduate has been named among the "100 Outstanding Alumni" of New York's State University System, is a member of the Judson Welliver Society of former White House speechwriters, and lives with his wife, Sarah, and two children in Rochester.